THE MOON EXPOSED

Allison Lassieur

www.raintreepublishers.co.uk

Visit our website to find out more information about **Raintree** books.

To order:
 Phone 44 (0) 1865 888112
Send a fax to 44 (0) 1865 314091
 Visit the Raintree bookshop at **www.raintreepublishers.co.uk** to browse our catalogue and order online.

First published in Great Britain by Raintree, Halley Court, Jordan Hill, Oxford OX2 8EJ, part of Harcourt Education.
Raintree is a registered trademark of Harcourt Education Ltd.

© Harcourt Education Ltd 2007
First published in paperback 2007
The moral right of the proprietor has been asserted.

Editorial: Nancy Dickmann and Harriet Milles
Design: Michelle Lisseter and Bigtop
Illustrations: Darren Lingard
Picture Research: Mica Brancic and Maria Joannou
Production: Camilla Crask

Originated by Modern Age
Printed and bound in China by WKT Company Limited

10-digit ISBN 1 406 20469 2 (hardback)
13-digit ISBN 978-1-4062-0469-8
11 10 09 08 07
10 9 8 7 6 5 4 3 2 1

10-digit ISBN 1 406 20494 3 (paperback)
13-digit ISBN 978-1-4062-0494-0
11 10 09 08 07
10 9 8 7 6 5 4 3 2 1

British Library Cataloguing in Publication Data
Lassieur, Allison
The moon exposed - (Fusion): The moon
523.3
A full catalogue record for this book is available from the British Library.

Acknowledgements
The author and publisher are grateful to the following for permission to reproduce copyright material: Corbis **pp. 5**, **28**; Corbis/The Image Bank **p. 11**; Masterfile **p. 13**; NASA **pp. 9** (Jet Propulsion Laboratory), **15** (Human Space Flight), **16**, **25** (Kennedy Space Center), **26** (Neil Armstrong), **29** (Edgar D. Mitchell); Science Photo Library **pp. 19** (NASA); **22–23** (John Sanford).

Cover photograph of the Moon reproduced with permission of Getty Images/Photodisc.

The publishers would like to thank Nancy Harris and Harold Pratt for their assistance in the preparation of this book.

Every effort has been made to contact copyright holders of any material reproduced in this book. Any omissions will be rectified in subsequent printings if notice is given to the publishers.

Disclaimer
All the Internet addresses (URLs) given in this book were valid at the time of going to press. However, due to the dynamic nature of the Internet, some addresses may have changed, or sites may have changed or ceased to exist since publication. While the author and publishers regret any inconvenience this may cause readers, no responsibility for any such changes can be accepted by either the author or the publishers.

It is recommended that adults supervise children on the Internet.

Contents

Some words are printed in bold, **like this**. You can find out what they mean on page 30. You can also look in the box at the bottom of the page where they first appear.

Fire in the Sky

People have always seen the Moon in the sky. Thousands of years ago, no one knew what the Moon was. So people made up stories to explain how the Moon came to be.

Some thought the Moon was a huge, spinning bowl of fire. Others believed the Moon was a mirror. They thought it **reflected** an image of Earth. Many people believed in powerful Moon gods and goddesses. Some thought a moon god watched over people as they travelled at night. Others thought a moon goddess brought good luck.

As time passed, people learned more about the Moon. They found out that the Moon is not a mirror. They found out it is not a bowl of fire. They found that the Moon is a natural **satellite** of Earth. That means it moves around Earth in a regular pattern.

reflect   bounce back
satellite   object that travels around a planet

◀Thousands of years ago, people wondered what the Moon was. Today we know a lot more about it.

What is the Moon?

The Moon is about four billion years old. It is round like Earth. But in other ways it is very different. The Moon is much smaller than Earth.

Almost four moons could fit into Earth. The **diameter**, or width, of the Moon is only 3,475 kilometres (2,159 miles). The diameter of Earth is 12,756 kilometres (7,926 miles).

The Moon looks bright in the sky. That is because it is the closest body to Earth. Only the Sun appears brighter. The Moon does not have light of its own. It **reflects** (bounces back) light from the Sun.

Moon myths

*Today people know a lot of facts about the Moon. But in the past they did not. So they made up **myths**, or stories, about the Moon. You will see some of these moon myths in this book. Read on to find out if any of them are true.*

diameter   width of a circle or ball
myth   story that explains something about the world

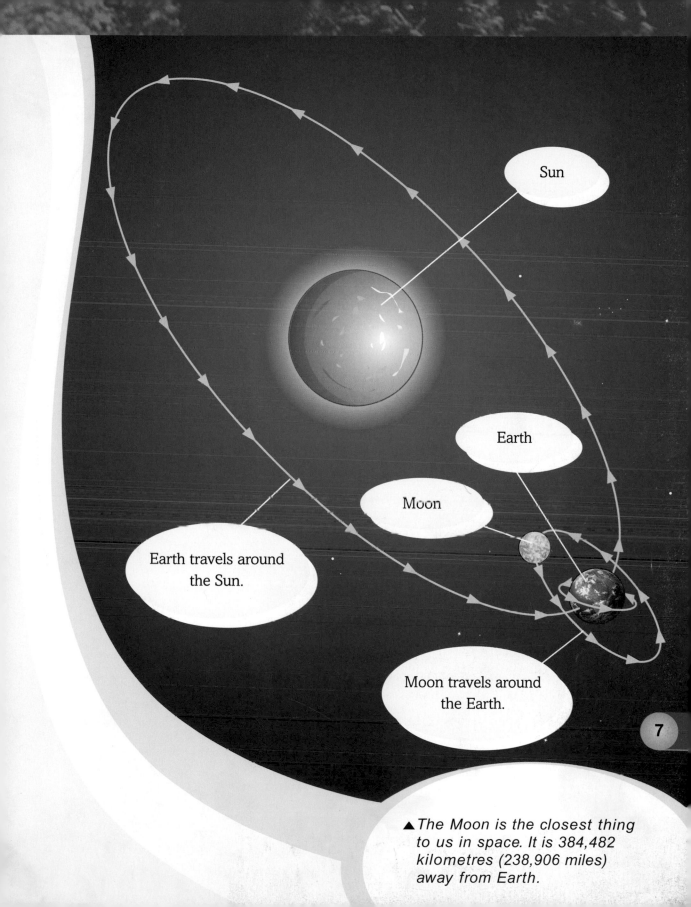

Sun

Earth

Moon

Earth travels around
the Sun.

Moon travels around
the Earth.

▲The Moon is the closest thing
to us in space. It is 384,482
kilometres (238,906 miles)
away from Earth.

Moon on the move

The Moon never sits still. It spins on its **axis**. An axis is an imaginary line. The Moon's axis runs through its centre. One full spin of the Moon takes $29\frac{1}{2}$ days. A spin is called a **rotation**. This means that one day on the Moon is as long as a month on Earth!

The Moon also **orbits** around Earth. To orbit means to travel in a circular path around an object. It takes $29\frac{1}{2}$ days for the Moon to make a full orbit around Earth. That is the same amount of time it takes the Moon to spin once on its axis.

Moon myths

A person or animal pulls the Moon across the sky. True or not true?

Moon myth: BUSTED!
Of course we know this is not true. But people used to believe this myth. Now we know more about the Moon. We know that the Moon's orbit makes it move across the sky.

axis   imaginary line that runs through the centre of a circle
orbit   travel in a circular path around an object
rotation   spinning or turning

▼ *The Moon takes about a month to orbit Earth.*

Moon-made motion

The Moon stays near Earth because of **gravity**. Gravity is a **force**. It pulls objects close to something. It makes things fall to the ground. It is also what keeps you on Earth. Without gravity, you would float into space!

Anything that has **mass** has its own gravity. Mass is how much there is of an object. The more mass an object has, the stronger its gravity.

The Moon has gravity. But the pull of gravity on the Moon is not very strong. If you dropped something on the Moon, it would fall very slowly. On the Moon, you can jump six times higher than you can on Earth.

Moon myths

A ring around the Moon means bad weather is coming. True or not true?

*Moon **myth**: TRUE. A ring happens when moonlight shines through ice crystals. The ice crystals are high up in Earth's **atmosphere**. The atmosphere is the layers of air around Earth. Those ice crystals might mean a storm is coming.*

atmosphere	layers of air around Earth
force	energy caused by motion
gravity	force of a body that pulls objects close to it
mass	how much there is of an object

11

▲ On the Moon, you could jump over cars!

The Moon and Earth

The Moon's **gravity** is always pulling on Earth. But Earth has a much bigger **mass** than the Moon. This means that Earth's gravity is stronger.

But Earth's oceans do feel the pull of the Moon's gravity. The Moon's gravity pulls the oceans towards it. This makes the oceans bulge, or get higher, in some places. These bulges are called **tides**. Tides are the rise or fall of the water in the oceans.

When these bulges reach their tallest height, it is called high tide. This bulge pulls water away from other areas of the ocean. The places where the water is pulled away become flat. In those places, it is low tide.

The bulges follow the Moon's **orbit** as it travels around Earth. This makes high and low tides happen in different places. There are two high tides each day at any one place. There are two low tides each day at any one place.

Moon myths

The tide is higher during a full moon. True or not true?

*Moon **myth**: BUSTED! A full moon does not affect the height of the tides.*

tide   rise and fall of the oceans

low tide

high tide

high tide

oceans

The pull of the Moon's gravity.

▶ In between the high tides are low tides.

low tide

▼ This is a beach at low tide. Can you see the high tide mark on the posts? That is how high the water gets at high tide.

high tide mark

13

What is on the Moon?

The Moon has many **craters**. A crater is a bowl-shaped hole. Some craters are very small. Others are very, very big. The biggest crater is called the South Pole-Aitken Basin. It is nearly 2,413 kilometres (1,500 miles) wide.

▼ The Moon's craters were made by chunks of rock flying through space. The rocks crashed into the Moon. They left craters where they hit the surface.

crater   hole shaped like a bowl

Moon myths

The Moon is made of green cheese. True or not true?

*Moon **myth**: BUSTED! There is no cheese on the Moon! Green cheese is cheese that isn't ready to eat yet. Long ago people thought the Moon looked like this kind of cheese.*

Most moon craters are named after famous scientists from the past. One crater is called Armstrong Crater. It was named after Neil Armstrong. He was the first person to walk on the Moon.

▼ This is a picture of the Moon's surface. It was taken on the Apollo 17 space mission. Can you see the **astronauts'** footprints?

Seas on the Moon?

Look at the Moon. You will see some dark areas. These dark areas are called maria. The word maria means "seas". A long time ago, people thought the dark areas were water. But maria are really huge areas of flat land.

The Moon's maria have different names. One is called *Mare Nubium*. This means "Sea of Clouds". Another is called *Mare Tranquillitatis*. It means "Sea of **Tranquility**". Tranquility means peacefulness.

Most maria have many ridges. The ridges look like small hills. Maria also have long, winding channels. They are called rilles. Rilles were made by running **lava**. Lava is hot, melted rock.

Moon myths

There is a man in the Moon. True or not true?

*Moon **myth**: BUSTED! When the Moon is full it might look like it has a smiling face. But this is because of the **craters**, maria, and ridges on the Moon's surface.*

astronaut	person trained to travel in space
lava	hot, melted rock
tranquility	peacefulness

Hot and cold Moon

The Moon does not have weather like Earth. There are no clouds or storms. But it gets very cold and very hot.

Earth's **atmosphere**, or layers of air, protects it from the Sun's heat. The Moon does not have an atmosphere. So parts of the Moon get very hot. It can get as hot as 110 °C (230 °F). The hottest day on Earth was only 58 °C (136 °F).

The Moon also gets very cold. This happens on the far side of the Moon. This side faces away from the Sun. There it can be as cold as -180 °C (-292 °F). That is cold enough for a person to freeze to death in a few seconds! On Earth, the coldest day ever was -89 °C (-129 °F).

▼ *This is a photo of the far side of the Moon. Until spacecraft could reach the Moon, people did not know what the far side looked like.*

Moon myths

Little green people live on the Moon. True or not true?

*Moon **myth**: BUSTED! We know that no creatures live on the Moon. One reason is that the Moon gets too cold and too hot. Nothing could survive there.*

Moon lights

The Moon does not make its own light. It **reflects** (bounces back) light from the Sun. As it **orbits** (moves around) Earth, part of the Moon is always facing the Sun.

As the Moon moves in its orbit, we can only see part of it. That is the part of the Moon that is facing the Sun. This is why the Moon looks like it is a different shape at different times of the month.

Watch the Moon for a few days. One day it is full and round. This is called a full moon. A week later, it looks much smaller. The Moon is not changing shape. It is going through its **phases**. These phases are the Moon's cycle.

Moon myths

Moon myth: A full moon makes people turn into werewolves. True or not true?

*Moon **myth**: BUSTED! There is no such thing as a werewolf!*

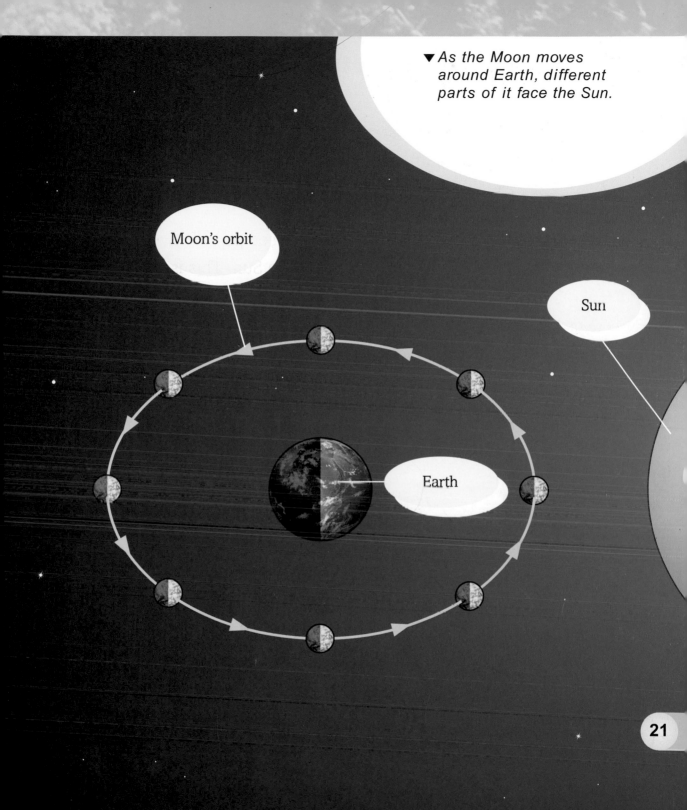

▼ As the Moon moves around Earth, different parts of it face the Sun.

Moon's orbit

Sun

Earth

Phases of the Moon

On some nights, a whole side of the Moon can be seen on Earth. That is a full moon. It looks round. Sometimes the Moon looks like the letter C. At other times it looks like a circle that is cut in half. The different shapes that we can see are the **phases** of the Moon.

2

Waxing crescent: You can see just less than half of the lit portion of the Moon.

1

New moon: The Moon's sunlit side is facing away from Earth.

4

Waxing **gibbous**: You can see more than $\frac{2}{3}$ of the lit half of the Moon.

3

First quarter: You can see the right half of the Moon.

gibbous swollen on one side
waning becoming smaller
waxing becoming larger

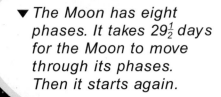

▼ *The Moon has eight phases. It takes 29½ days for the Moon to move through its phases. Then it starts again.*

5

Full moon:
The Moon's fully lit side faces Earth.

6

Waning gibbous:
You can see less of the lit side of the Moon.

7

Last quarter:
You can see only half of the lit portion of the Moon.

8

Waning crescent:
The Moon looks like the letter C. Soon it will be the new moon phase again.

Where did the Moon go?

Sometimes the Moon, the Sun, and Earth line up in a certain way. When this happens, Earth blocks the Sun's light. The light does not reach the Moon. That makes the Moon seem to disappear. This is called an **eclipse**.

Earth's shadow slowly creeps across the full moon. In a few minutes it covers the Moon. The Moon disappears. But Earth's shadow keeps moving. Soon the full moon is back again.

There is a full moon every month. Why is there not an eclipse every month? Usually Earth does not block the Sun's light from the Moon. But every so often Earth lines up between the Sun and the Moon. Then an eclipse will happen.

Moon myths

A full moon disappears because it has been swallowed by an animal. True or not true?

*Moon **myth**: BUSTED! In the past, people did not understand what an eclipse was. They invented stories to explain it. Now people know the Moon is still there. It is just hidden by Earth's shadow.*

24

eclipse   when a body in space partly or fully blocks another

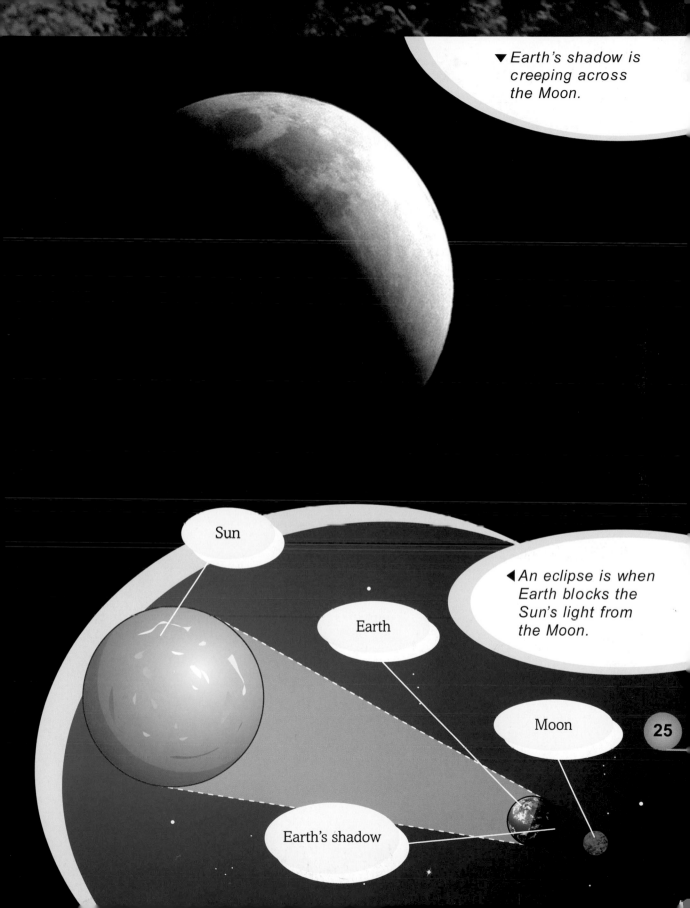

▼ *Earth's shadow is creeping across the Moon.*

Sun

Earth

◀ *An eclipse is when Earth blocks the Sun's light from the Moon.*

Moon

25

Earth's shadow

A walk on the Moon

For thousands of years, people wondered what the Moon really looked like. In 1969 they found out. That year, three **astronauts** travelled to the Moon. Their mission was called Apollo 11.

Neil Armstrong was the first person to walk on the Moon. Then Buzz Aldrin joined him. The third astronaut on the trip was Michael Collins. He stayed on the ship.

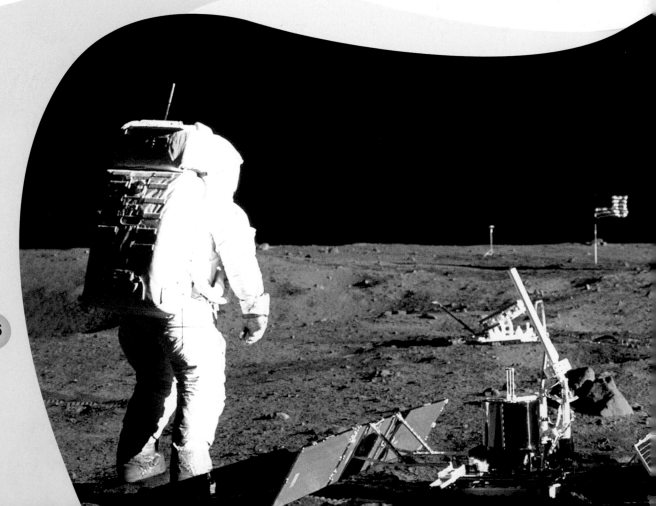

Every time the astronauts walked on the Moon, they bounced! That is because there is not as much **gravity** on the Moon as on Earth. But their space suits were very heavy. They did not bounce very far.

The astronauts stayed at the Moon for about a day. They collected more than 23 kilograms (50 pounds) of Moon dirt and rocks. They took a lot of pictures.

Moon myths busted!

Scientists from around the world studied the samples from the Moon. They looked at the pictures. They learned many things. They found out how old the Moon is. They found out how the Moon was formed. They were able to "bust" many moon **myths**.

◀ Neil Armstrong took this picture of Buzz Aldrin while they were on the Moon.

Moon tourists

Astronauts took more than just their space suits into space. Each astronaut was allowed to take along a few things. Here are some that found their way into space.

Apollo 14 astronaut Alan Shepard took golf balls to the Moon. He put a golf club head on a tool handle. Then he played golf on the Moon!

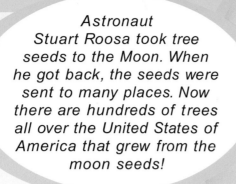

Astronaut Stuart Roosa took tree seeds to the Moon. When he got back, the seeds were sent to many places. Now there are hundreds of trees all over the United States of America that grew from the moon seeds!

Neil Armstrong took a United States flag to the Moon. It still stands on the Moon today.

The last visit to the Moon happened in 1972. Today scientists are planning a new Moon visit. What things would you take to the Moon?

Glossary

astronaut person trained to travel in space. Three astronauts went to the Moon on Apollo 11.

atmosphere layers of air around Earth. The oxygen you breathe is in the Earth's atmosphere.

axis imaginary line that runs through the centre of a circle. Earth's axis runs through the North Pole and the South Pole.

crater hole shaped like a bowl. When space rocks hit the Moon, they made craters.

diameter width of a circle or ball. The diameter of the Moon is 3,475 kilometres (2,159 miles).

eclipse when a body in space partly or fully blocks another

force energy caused by motion. The force that pulls objects to Earth is called gravity.

gibbous swollen on one side. One phase of the Moon is called the gibbous.

gravity force of a body that pulls objects close to it. The Moon's gravity causes tides.

lava hot, melted rock. Some features on the Moon were made by lava.

mass how much there is of an object. The Earth has a very large mass.

myth story that explains something about the world. For thousands of years, people told myths to explain things about the Moon.

orbit travel in a circular path around an object. It takes one year for the Earth to orbit the Sun.

phase one part of a cycle. The Moon moves through eight phases during a month.

reflect bounce back. The Moon's surface reflects light from the Sun.

rotation spinning or turning. Earth makes a full rotation once every 24 hours.

satellite object that travels around a planet. The Moon is Earth's natural satellite.

tide rise and fall of the oceans

tranquility peacefulness. The Sea of Tranquility is a flat area of the Moon.

waning becoming smaller. When the Moon is waning, you see less and less of it.

waxing becoming larger. When the Moon is waxing, you see more and more of it.

Want to know more?

Books to read

- *The First Moon Landing*, by Gillian Clements (Franklin Watts, 2002).

- *Kingfisher Young Explore: Solar System*, by Mike Goldsmith (Kingfisher, 2004).

- *The Moon*, by Dr. Raman K. Prinja (Heinemann Library, 2002)

Websites

- http://science.nasa.gov/headlines/y2002/13aug_Moontrees.htm
  Find out where the "moon trees" were planted after the Apollo 14 mission.

- http://teacher.scholastic.com/researchtools/articlearchives/space/Moon.htm
  Visit this site for lots more answers to questions about the Moon.

- http://starchild.gsfc.nasa.gov/docs/StarChild/StarChild.html
  For more information about the Sun, the planets, and other parts of the universe.

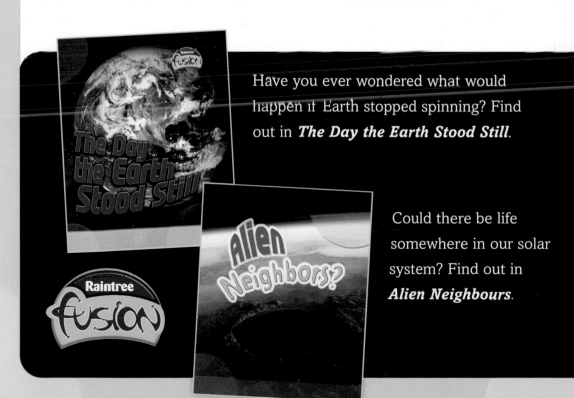

Have you ever wondered what would happen if Earth stopped spinning? Find out in **The Day the Earth Stood Still**.

Could there be life somewhere in our solar system? Find out in *Alien Neighbours*.

Index